It's Not Catching

Broken Bones

Heinemann
LIBRARY

www.heinemann.co.uk/library
Visit our website to find out more information about **Heinemann Library** books.

To order:
☎ Phone 44 (0) 1865 888066
🖹 Send a fax to 44 (0) 1865 314091
💻 Visit the Heinemann Bookshop at www.heinemann.co.uk/library to browse our catalogue and order online.

First published in Great Britain by Heinemann Library, Halley Court, Jordan Hill, Oxford OX2 8EJ, part of Harcourt Education.
Heinemann is a registered trademark of Harcourt Education Ltd.

Editorial: Sarah Eason and Kathy Peltan
Design: Dave Oakley, Arnos Design
Picture Research: Helen Reilly, Arnos Design
Artwork: Tower Designs UK Ltd p.14;
    Nick Hawken p.24.
Production: Edward Moore

Originated by Dot Gradations Ltd
Printed and bound in Hong Kong and China by South China Printing Company

The paper used to print this book comes from sustainable sources.

ISBN 0 431 02145 7 (hardback)
08 07 06 05 04
10 9 8 7 6 5 4 3 2 1

ISBN 0 431 02154 6 (paperback)
09 08 07 06 05
10 9 8 7 6 5 4 3 2 1

British Library Cataloguing in Publication Data
Royston, Angela
Broken bones. – (It's not catching)
617.1'5

A full catalogue record for this book is available from the British Library.

Acknowledgements
The publishers would like to thank the following for permission to reproduce photographs: Alamy/Image100 p. **6**; Getty Images/VCL/Spencer Rowell p. **13**; John Walmsley pp. **18**, **22**; Phillip James Photography pp. **5**, **8**, **9**, **10**, **11**, **20**, **21**, **27**, **28**, **29**; Powerstock/Robert J. Bennett p. **12**; Rubberball Productions p. **4**; SPL/CC Studio p. **26**; SPL/Custom Medical Stock Photo p. **7**; SPL/Dept. of Clinical Radiology, Salisbury p. **16**; SPL/Dr P. Marazzi p. **17**; SPL/Jim Selby p. **23**; SPL/Scott Camazine p. **19**; The Wellcome Trust p. **15**; Trevor Clifford p. **25**.

Cover photograph reproduced with permission of Corbis.

The publishers would like to thank David Wright for his assistance in the preparation of this book.

Every effort has been made to contact copyright holders of any material reproduced in this book. Any omissions will be rectified in subsequent printings if notice is given to the publishers.

Contents

Words written in bold, **like this**, are explained
in the Glossary.

What is a broken bone?

Bones are the hard bits inside your body that make up your **skeleton**. Bones give your body its shape. They also support your head and other parts of your body.

Bones are strong, but sometimes a bone can crack or break. When a bone is **injured**, it is too painful to move properly or to put your weight on.

Who gets broken bones?

Anyone can break one of their **bones**.
But people who are very active or rush
around without thinking are more likely
to have an **accident**.

Adults' bones become more **brittle** as they grow very old. Old people, particularly women, can easily break a bone. But broken bones are not catching.

Twisting your ankle

When you are running around, it's very easy to turn your **ankle** over. Your ankle suddenly gives way, or you may twist your foot as you land.

Twisting your ankle is not usually serious and the pain soon goes away. But if your ankle swells up, you have probably **sprained** it or even broken a **bone**.

Falling

When you fall awkwardly, you can knock and **jolt** a **bone**. A bad jolt can crack or break the bone.

Falling on to a hard surface, such as **concrete**, will jolt your bones. Falling off somewhere high above the ground jolts your bones too.

serious accidents

Sometimes people are involved in serious **accidents**, such as car crashes. Sometimes people are killed in car crashes. Others may have one or more **bones** broken.

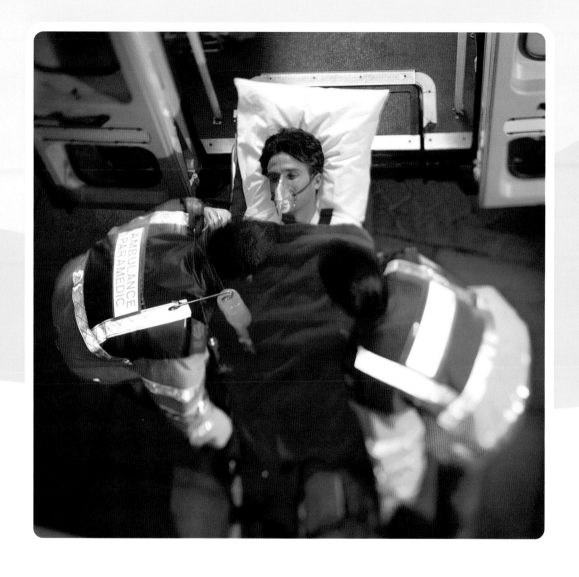

Being run over is another kind of serious
accident. Being hit by a moving car or other
vehicle is likely to break a person's bones and
hurt them very badly.

Sprains

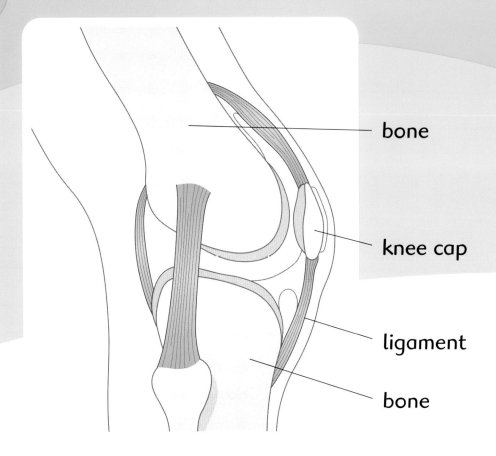

bone

knee cap

ligament

bone

A **joint** is where two or more **bones** meet.
Ligaments are stretchy bands that hold the
joint together. A joint is **sprained** when a
ligament is torn or stretched.

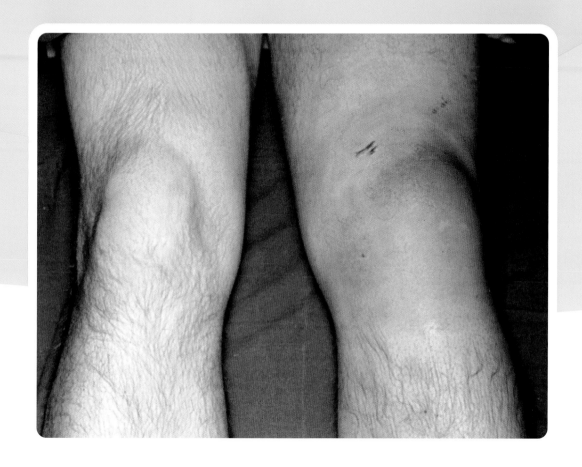

When a ligament is damaged, the joint is very painful. It quickly becomes swollen. Trying to move the joint makes the pain even worse.

Dislocated joints

dislocated joint

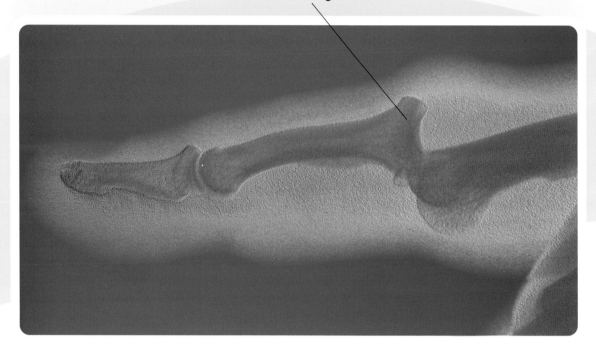

In a **joint** the ends of the **bones** fit together. In some **accidents** a bone is pulled out of position. It is said to be **dislocated**.

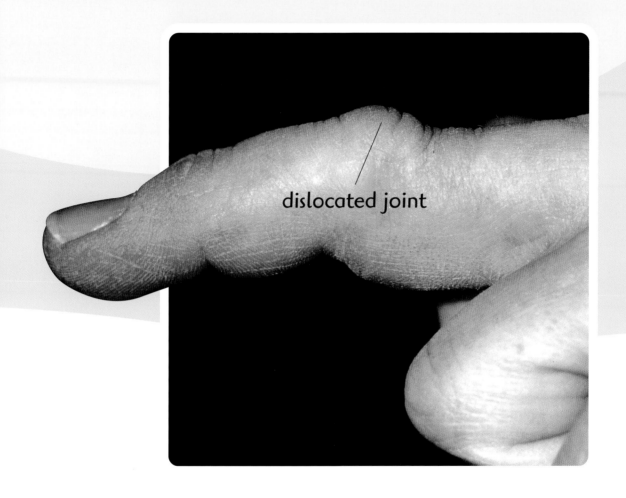

dislocated joint

You can tell if a joint is dislocated because its shape looks wrong. The joint is very painful to move or to touch.

Broken bones

An **accident** can crack a **bone** or break it all the way through. Only an **X-ray** can show where and how a bone is damaged.

broken bones

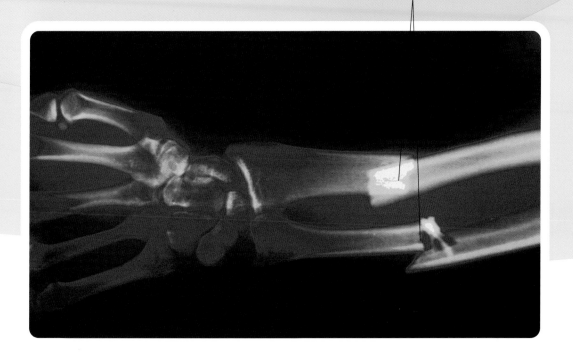

An X-ray machine takes a photograph of the **injured** bones. This X-ray shows someone's arm. Two of the bones are clearly broken.

Treating an injured joint

The best treatment for a **sprained joint** is to rest it while the **injured ligament** heals itself. A stretchy bandage helps to support the joint while it heals.

If a joint is **dislocated**, a doctor will move the **bones** back into the correct position. As the joint gets better and stops hurting, you should exercise it gently. This boy is circling his foot to exercise his ankle.

Treating a broken bone

A broken bone needs to be protected while it **heals**. An **X-ray** shows where the bone is injured. Then a wet bandage is wound around it.

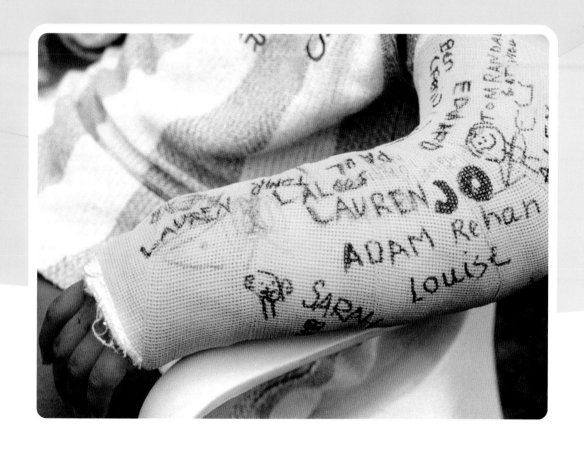

The bandage contains a special substance. As the bandage dries, the substance hardens. It forms a strong **cast** that protects the bone and joint.

How a broken bone mends

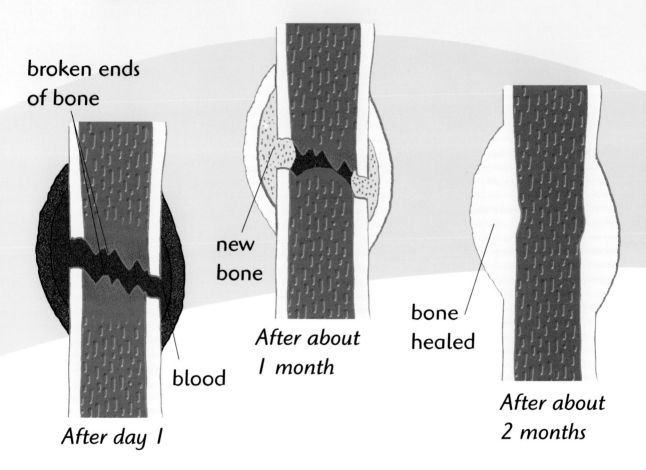

broken ends of bone

blood

After day 1

new bone

After about 1 month

bone healed

After about 2 months

A broken or cracked **bone** mends itself. Blood seals the break and forms a **clot**. Slowly new bone grows between the break in the bone.

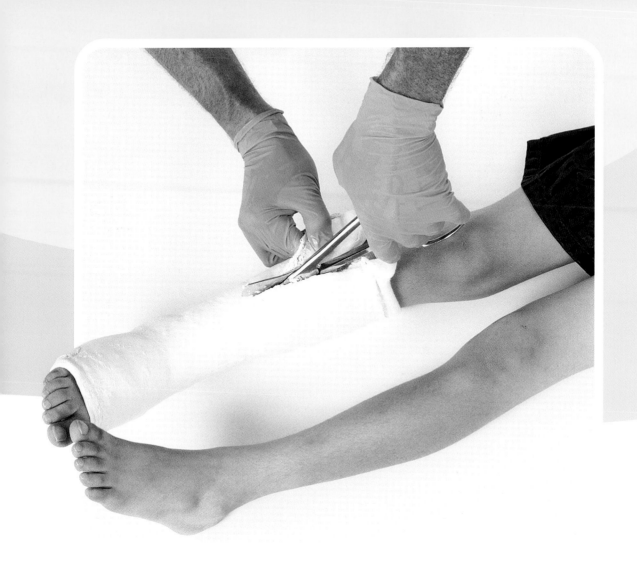

It takes about two months or longer until the ends of the bone have joined and the bone is strong again. Then the **cast** is removed.

Getting strong again

When a **cast** is removed, the **muscles** that move the **joint** have become very weak. A **physiotherapist** gives you exercises to make the muscles strong again.

The muscles are weak
because you could not use
them while the joint was in
the cast. You have to do the
exercises at home every day
for several weeks.

preventing accidents

The best way to prevent **accidents** is to be careful! When you are climbing, always move one hand or foot at a time. Don't jump off high places.

Be particularly careful when you are crossing a road. Cross at safe places, such as traffic lights or **zebra crossings**. Look both ways before you cross.

Glossary

accident   something that happens by mistake

ankle   joint between your lower leg and
your foot

brittle   easily broken

bone   hard substance that makes up
the skeleton

cast   hard shell made from fibreglass or plaster
that protects a broken bone while it heals

clot   soft lump of thickened blood

concrete   hard substance made from sand,
gravel, cement and water

dislocated   out of place

heal   to mend, or become healthy again

injured   hurt or damaged

joint   place where two or more bones meet and
which allows one bone to move without
the other

jolt   sudden shock or knock

ligament   stretchy band that holds a joint together

muscles parts of the body that move the bones or flesh

physiotherapist person who uses exercises to help injured or weak muscles become strong

skeleton all the bones in the body

sprain when a ligament is damaged by twisting or stretching it too far

X-ray kind of photograph that shows the bones and some other parts inside the body

zebra crossing part of the road marked with black and white stripes where vehicles should stop to let you cross the road

More books to read

It's My Body: Arms and Hands, Lola Schaefer, (Raintree, 2003)

Look After Yourself: Get Some Exercise, Angela Royston, (Heinemann Library, 2003)

Safe and Sound: Safety First, Angela Royston, (Heinemann Library, 2001)

Why Do Bones Break? And Other Questions About Movement, Angela Royston, (Heinemann Library, 2003)

Index